Why Are They Like That?
Disabled People

Questions you've dared to ask, answered
by real people, celebrities and experts

A book series based on the award-winning
sharing project that's captured worldwide
attention helping people in their personal,
social and business relationships

I0441918

Phillip J. Milano

For Robin, Jacob, Lucas and Ben

Publisher:
Y Forum
yforum@yforum.com

ISBN: 978-1-07-977975-2

Cover and interior layout by Sandy Weber,
Key 3 Creative, Jacksonville, Florida
Cover photo credit: Rawpixel. Stock photo for illustrative purposes
only; any person depicted is a posed model.

Content based in part on the popular Y? sharing project and Dare
to Ask column

Find out more about the author, upcoming books and speeches at
www.phillipmilano.com, www.facebook.com/PhillipJMilano or
@PhillipMilano.

Books In This Series

Praise for the Y? sharing project and the book "I Can't Believe You Asked That!" (Perigee)

"Milano is quietly revolutionizing cross-cultural communication..."
- Pulitzer Prize-winning columnist Leonard Pitts

"If you've ever hesitated to ask a question because you think it might be considered insensitive or impolitic, now is your chance ... Nothing is considered out of bounds..."
- CNN Headline News

"(It) tells more about who we are and how we feel about each other than you're likely to learn from a dozen sociology texts..."
- Washington Post News Service

"Mr. Milano has dared to open the field of debate to the maximum…"
- Le Monde, Paris

"(A) remarkable contribution to cross-cultural understanding…"
- The (London) Guardian

"A truly rare achievement … has the potential to have a profound impact on the way we all see and understand each other..."
- Playboy magazine

"It's an incredible book. It diffuses everything ... Nothing is off limits, and the questions have that childlike honesty to them..."
- Dee Snider, Twisted Sister; host, "Dee Snider Radio"

"A take-no-prisoners attitude prevails between the volume's covers . . . This book is hard to put down..."
- Midwest Book Review

"A+ (highest rating) … Everything you wanted to know but were afraid to ask gets tackled here ..."
- Entertainment Weekly

CONTENTS

Introduction

Why Are They Like That? is a series of books based on an award-winning worldwide sharing project in which real people, experts and celebrities talk about things that make us different from each other. Silly things. Sad things. Funny things. Profound things.

Read with an open mind and we believe that by the time you're finished you'll have a much better understanding of how to make more and real friends, money and love. It's that simple.

Why? Because this isn't about trying to get ahead with diversity training. We are well beyond that. According to the Census Bureau, by 2050 the United States will have no racial or ethnic minority.

No, this is about moving past talking about how to understand each other to talking to each other. Right now.

That's why there's no agenda to these books other than getting the conversation going. We can discuss studies and methods for elevating social consciousness all we want, but there is no substitute for real dialogue.

That's where Why Are They Like That? stands apart from other books on the topic. You will see how people talk about their real differences of race, religion, sex, disability and more.

The success of the approach is proven: It's based on the ground-breaking Y? website project, blog and column that have attracted millions of visitors and worldwide media attention.

Our hope is that by reading, you will become more comfortable asking and answering the questions yourself, expecting the unexpected in return and helping change the ground rules for how we learn from and about each other. To that end, we wrap up each book in the series with our O.U.T.L.O.U.D. Method for Dialogue, with tips to help you get your own conversations started. Ultimately, that is what this effort is all about.

After all, if you want to make more friends, money and love, you better know the people you're talking to, selling to or opening to. Knowledge isn't just power. It's all power.

Enjoy.

Phillip J. Milano
Founder, Y?

How useful is braille at an ATM?

They asked:

Why do drive-through ATM machines have braille on the buttons?

Nick, Moscow, Idaho

You said::

Haven't you ever backed up to an ATM so your passenger could use it?

Cindy, Lansing, Mich.

A better question would be why they don't have instructions posted in braille or aren't required to speak instructions. Each ATM has a different button arrangement, and some of the buttons are not brailled because they serve multiple uses. I used to have a blind significant other, and this made him angry. The people who try to "adopt" these things need to do a much better job of consulting the blind.

John, Chicago

My wife is blind. It's simply cost-effective to make all of the panels the same, whether they are for "drive-up" ATMs or not.

Mark, 35, Boca Raton

We found:

Please take your information below. Thank you for reading. Have A Great Day!

Chris Kuell, blind writer, second-vice president of the National Federation of the Blind of Connecticut:

Banks put the braille on all ATMs to try to comply with the Americans with Disabilities Act of 1990, which required that the machines be "independently usable by people with vision impairments."

"It was done to show they were being good citizens, when in fact it didn't help a blind person because we can't read the digital display," Kuell said.

Rob Evans, former director of global industry marketing for ATM-maker NCR:

"Why do drive-up ATMs have braille? Good question. It's almost as if we're saying, 'If you made it that far, by golly that's the least we could do.' That's a flip answer, but the real reason is there are distinct differences among visually impaired people ... a small segment are active in the workforce, say, and may drive to work in taxis [sitting behind the driver] and don't want to give their debit card and secret code to someone else."

These braille ATMs aren't really accessible, however, unless a blind user knows what each button does — which eventually led to ATMs with headphone jacks and speech output software. Those came along in the 2000s from makers like NCR and Diebold. Users just plug in their headphone set and they're in business.

Julie Davis, former spokeswoman for Bank of America:

The company operates more than 7,000 "Talking ATMs." It expects the majority of its locations will have voice-guided ATMs.

Why go through all this for a small group of people? According to Kuell, "There's also a spillover benefit: maybe the guys who design microwaves, or home heating, etc., will see that a bank or Publix thought about this, and think, 'Maybe I ought to think about this the next time I design my product.'

"It's a cue to everybody else: the ADA guidelines work. You just don't know when a person might need them, just as you don't know when you install it if a blind person might need to use a drive-through ATM."

She aches for young people to 'get' arthritis

They asked:

Do younger people understand how age-related diseases like arthritis affect someone's lifestyle, even if they're not in a wheelchair? I sometimes feel my illnesses are not quite accepted or believed.

Martha, 59, Portage, Mich.

You said::

Yes. My older sister found out she had arthritis in her wrists when she was 23. She is a drafter and works on a computer every day. Some days she has to wear a wristband, and others it is almost impossible to work due to the pain.

BeBe, 23, female, Eglin, Fla.

I used to be puzzled at my folks when they talked about arthritis, but I developed it and was shocked. Try getting a prescription for Celebrex from a doctor or insurance company at age 17.

Jeff, 25, Richmond, Va.

We found:

Hey kids! About 300,000 of you in the United States have juvenile arthritis! Get hip to joint pain with the wisdom of the No. 1 Super Villain of all time! Or else!

Our first go-round ringing up Darth Vader resulted in hearing only some breaths on the other end of the phone. Then it went dead. We're not kidding. Long-distance calls can be complicated, we know, but we got scared and felt a death pinch headed our way. We got up the courage to dial again, though.

Finally we got British weight-lifting champ David Prowse, the mountain inside that black cape and helmet for the first three "Star Wars" films. He's had rheumatoid arthritis since at least age 13. He spent more than a year imprisoned in a hospital room in "leg irons," as he called them. Years later, in his 60s, he discovered he had septic arthritis. Among numerous other procedures, the 78-year-old actor has had both hips replaced.

He's determined his youthful joint pain was from "growing too fast" — he was 6 foot 5 by 15 — but now advocates for arthritis awareness, bringing it up in his bio "Straight From the Force's Mouth."

His athleticism and physique shielded him from a lot of ribbing about his joint problems as a youth, but kids can be cruel toward others if they don't understand things, he said.

"They should know the causes, which in kids can sometimes be bad diet more than anything else," he said. "Or you can get it later on if you start damaging yourself. You bugger your knees up or get hurt in football and don't take any notice of it. The aches and pains go away, but tt catches up with you later."

If young people realized it's inflammation that can't be seen, they'd be less unsympathetic toward older people — and less likely to get it themselves, he noted.

"They'd exercise more sensibly, not strain themselves and keep their joints well-lubricated. A little cod liver oil every day really does help."

(Researchers at the U.K.'s Dundee University report that two teaspoons of cod liver oil a day decreases the amount of powerful painkillers needed to cut arthritis pain. New therapeutic medications come online almost every month.)

Still, we sense a disturbance in The Force. Really, was Lord Vader popping fish pills on the "Star Wars" set between repping the Empire in all those lightsaber duels with Luke and Obi-Wan?

"Oh I was fine on the set; my arthritis didn't show up until years later. I also had a stuntman when they thought the fighting was too complicated or that I'd fall off the gantry."

Are some 'disabled' cart riders faking it?

They asked:

What I just experienced at the grocery store infuriated me. Three women — a teenager, an elderly woman and a middle-aged woman — were shopping together. The teenager was riding a motorized cart for handicapped customers. After checking out, the teenager jumped off the cart and all three walked out laughing their butts off. I can understand teenage immaturity, but what about the others? What can managers and customers do?

Shirley, 50, St. Louis

You said::

Are you sure the teen didn't have a disability? My 22-year-old niece has a medical issue that makes it impossible for her to walk more than 10 to 15 minutes. She doesn't look disabled and can walk fine, but unless you knew her you wouldn't think she had an issue.

M., female, Georgia

As a handicapped shopper, I know that all people with a valid handicap will have a red (temporary) or blue (permanent) parking placard allowing them to use a handicap parking spot. A handicap registration goes with the placard. The handicapped person is to keep a copy of this registration on them at all times. If all stores had the available manpower, they should only issue carts to shoppers with a current handicap registration.

Rob, 49, Jacksonville

We found:

Art Metrano played a goofy cop in the "Police Academy" movies of the '80s — OK there were a lot of goofy cops in "Police Academy," but he was one of the more high-ranking ones.

Though he recovered after a fall from a ladder at home injured his spinal cord, he still uses a motorized wheelchair for longer distances, and advocates for the disabled.

Like his character, Metrano's not too subtle.

"Some of these people, they're thoughtless. … A young person who's never had any tragedy, they don't think about the other person as much. They see an electric cart and think, 'Oh there's something I can have, who gives a shit?' They don't care."

Metrano's plan for them?

"If I was physically able, I'd get out of my own cart and throw the kid off it and make sure it's there for someone who needs it."

But what about the rest of us? Or a store manager?

Placards in the carts' baskets reminding shoppers who the carts are really for would be a start — along with some firm assertiveness, he said.

"It's very delicate for a manager, but at the same time, if they see a young boy using one and he looks OK, they can ask the boy or his parent, 'Are you handicapped?' " said Metrano. "Don't just let the parent let the kid use it as a toy."

Metrano, whose one-man show "Jews Don't Belong On Ladders … An Accidental Comedy" has raised more than $175,000 for the Project Support for Spinal Cord Injury, is somewhat of a zealot when it comes to handicapped parking spots, too.

"I've had many occasions where I stopped someone in the lot. Once I even stopped a guy in L.A. that I knew. I said 'What are you doing with a handicapped spot?' He was like, 'I had an ingrown toenail removed.' Now that's stupid."

Deaf people: Ever just want to scream? So, do you?

They asked:

Do deaf people scream when they are frustrated?

Ezzie, 52, Pittsburgh

You said::

Although I don't, I had a deaf special-needs roommate who did. Man, what a howler!

Ashley, 24, deaf, St. Augustine

Deaf people have a "voice box" in their throat. They can make sounds perfectly or awfully. We are human beings, nothing more or less.

Stephen, 19, deaf, Clark, N.J.

I'm a deaf education/American Sign Language interpretation major. Deaf people react the same way to situations hearing people do. … except they do not always know they've made noises.

Christy, 22, Jacksonville

Deaf people do not scream when they are frustrated. No more than you or I do as people who can hear.

Sarah, Rochester, N.Y.

My parents are deaf. Some deaf people are quiet, by choice. Others don't care what they sound like and are very expressive vocally.

Kristina, 37, Seattle

I tend to internalize frustration so as not to bother other people. The answer may also depend on where I am at the time. I won't scream if frustrated at work.

Ray, deaf, Iowa

My sister lost her hearing at a very young age. When we were children, when she was in a room by herself, she would "utter" quite spontaneously, and yes, the volume did elevate with excitement.

Ed, Richmond, Va.

I teach at a school for the deaf. Often someone without hearing has well-developed vocal cords and uses them as frequently as anyone else.

Robert, 54, Portland, Ore.

We found:

Read our lips: When you gotta scream, you gotta scream.

"Many deaf people yell; it's a pent-up discharge that everyone needs as part of their neurological wiring," said psychologist Deborah Serani, an adjunct professor at Adelphi University in New York who specializes in depression and has worked with deaf people for more than 20 years. "It's not good to hold things in; it can lead to things like high blood pressure."

Just like hearing people, their facial expressions can get exaggerated, too, and they can shake their hands or tap a table to show frustration, she said.

"One [deaf] woman I was working with, she got extremely angry talking about a situation at work. ... She stood up and stamped her feet and was signing in such a large way that the lampshade on my desk started to shake. She pointed to it, and we both laughed."

Overemphasized signing and more expansive gesticulations can be typical for deaf people when frustrated, she added.

"One of my favorites is a word you can't print (sure we can: "asshole"), for someone they're upset with ... picture them, when mad, taking their hand, making a fist, and instead of keeping it tight, which they might do if mildly upset, opening it very wide so you can see a big O — like a sphincter."

We hear that one, loud and clear.

Violent, mentally ill ... and is his psychiatrist to blame?

They asked:

I befriended a paranoid schizophrenic, and he's accused my mother of saying something bad about him. I protested and he pulled a knife and threatened to stab me. His parents said he doesn't take his medication and drinks, which makes him irrational or violent. Could his psychiatrist be held responsible for his actions?

Tony, 41, Bronx, N.Y.

You said::

I've been surviving with a schizoaffective disorder 17 years. Your friend is responsible for his own actions unless he's a minor.

Jim, 35, Knoxville, Tenn.

What a horror. You need to talk to a lawyer or someone at your local police station.

Laurie B., Boston

Can he be "sectioned" (involuntary committal)? In Canada ... a person is committed if they are a "danger to themselves or others."

Ana, 37, Langley, Canada

I went with a man with the same disorder. He was always accusing. The relationship was over quickly. But he had a hard time accepting it and kept calling me. It can be painful when you feel nobody is around, but unfortunately they bring their trouble on themselves. They need a strong person to help with a hand up.

Mary, Green Cove Springs, Fla.

We found:

Generally, if you're diagnosed with schizophrenia or another serious mental illness, you're still legally responsible for your behavior, said Ron Honberg, legal director for the National Alliance on Mental Illness.

Exception: Let's say the person really deteriorates. All states have laws that let people be involuntarily committed if they're deemed a danger to themselves or others, or are gravely disabled, Honberg said. Or, they may be adjudged incompetent enough that they need a legal guardian.

So is that guardian culpable for someone else's violence? Not usually, but if they knew the person was going to behave violently, could have prevented it and did nothing, some courts have held them accountable.

As far as doctors, they generally aren't criminally liable, either. In one case in California, however, a guy told his psychiatrist he was going to off his ex-girlfriend, and the caregiver didn't warn the woman. After she was killed, her family won a civil judgment against the doctor because the court found he had a "duty to warn," Honberg said.

There's also the issue of psychiatric malpractice, but it's rare to win a case against a doctor unless he or she makes an "egregious departure" from accepted practice, he said.

All in all, the best way to respond to a violent situation is to get caregivers and local authorities involved early on, said Julia Shimizu of California, whose 25-year-old son is diagnosed with schizophrenia.

"One time, our neighbors had to call the police ... they came and were able to de-escalate things because they had received proper training. That works miracles. And it couldn't have happened if I hadn't created a relationship with police in advance."

Getting a read on how deaf people read

They asked:

When I read or write, I hear the words in my mind. How do the deaf do it?

Lonnie, El Paso, Texas

You said::

When I read, I "feel" the words in my mind. Depending on schooling, etc., we often learn written English as a second language, since American Sign Language is not related to English.

Anna, 30, deaf, Seattle

I don't hear the words, although I could speak. If I read a book, I try to visualize the story. For praying, I either sign in my mind or think the words. I used to dream in sign language (or gestures from those who don't know sign language) when I was a child. Now I dream in telepathy in place of gestures.

Christy, deaf, Michigan

Research suggests deaf people who have some ability to phonologically encode letters and words are the best readers. This usually means that deaf readers with some residual hearing are better readers.

Terry, 48, deaf female, Fremont, Calif.

We found:

Here's what's needed to read, whether you're deaf or not, said Barbara Schirmer, provost at Defiance College in Ohio and former professor of education at the University of Detroit Mercy, who studies how to improve outcomes for deaf readers:

"You have to be able to identify words, read them fluently and comprehend them," said Schirmer, author of "Language and Literacy Development in Children Who Are Deaf."

Using phonics — sounding out the words — is a key to more rapidly learning and remembering words. Even some profoundly deaf can learn phonics, she said.

For those who can't, kinesthetic methods can mimic phonics, such as feeling inside the throat or touching a deaf student's hand to the speaker's throat, she said.

Failing that, a newer strategy is to make sounds visual, in which hand signals coincide with the different letters and sounds in written words. That helps memorization.

"The job of a deaf child is to develop a store of words they can recognize by sight. That creates automatic word recognition."

It's not easy.

"The best analogy I've heard is that it's not like riding a bike, but more like playing baseball," Schirmer said. "Baseball consists of learning the skills, running the bases, catching, hitting, pitching ... you could be good at all, but still be lousy at baseball, because it's about the whole game. You have to put it all together."

In reading, the "click" happens when you move beyond identifying the words to comprehending what they mean together. That is the hardest part.

"The average deaf student graduates high school at a fourth- or fifth-grade reading level; it's been that way many years," she said. "Lots become wonderful readers, but it's a challenge."

Standing tall (and having sex) with someone's face in your chest

They asked::

As a short person, I've always wondered: What is it like to be tall?

C.P., 21, female, Montreal

You said::

I am 6 feet tall. If I go to a concert, I always have a good view. I can reach the top shelf at the supermarket, and when I was pregnant, I hardly showed. However, with dating, it used to be a problem. As a teenager, when I used to get asked to dance, the guy's face would fall when I stood up. Nevertheless, my fiance and the father to my child is only 5 feet 5. We get pointed at in the street, which I find funny.

Sarah, Ennis, Ireland

I'm 6 feet 3. My pant inseam needs to be 38 inches; that isn't easy to find. I also need a sleeve length of 37 inches. So clothes are always a challenge. Finding a comfortable car isn't easy. But I like being able to see (and be seen) over a crowd. I can pack on a little extra weight, and it isn't so noticeable since I'm vertically enhanced!

Mark, 38, Dallas

For men, being taller has many advantages, whereas the opposite would apply for women.

Christopher, 23, Arlington, Texas

Christopher: why would it not be an advantage for women to be taller? I am tall and really enjoy it. I don't feel vulnerable or intimidated by men, and I have no trouble getting partners. OK, so small women have a wider choice of partners (if you like men taller than you), but there's enough to go 'round, you know.

Beth, 24, United Kingdom

We found:

We can't list all the ups and downs (that'd be a tall order), but here are some from 6-foot-3 Arianne Cohen, TV producer and author of "The Tall Book" and "The Sex Diaries Project."

Ups: Tall people get noticed in the workplace, earn more (about $789 per inch per year), can eat 3 billion or so more calories per lifetime (about 100,000 servings of ice cream), live longer on average, are a tad smarter (factors that lead to taller, healthier bodies also make for healthier brains) and, if men, enjoy a dating boon because women tend to be attracted to height.

Downs: Tall people get noticed in the workplace, live in an alienating world that doesn't fit them (think city buses and public toilets), have a hard time finding clothes that work (the only major women's retailer is Long Tall Sally) and have lower birth rates (tall females usually want to "date up" and have trouble finding a taller mate). They also see a lot of dirt and grime because few people clean above about 6 feet or so.

Oh, and though it's not related to height, tall men can feel under-endowed.

"If you're average in that department, but it's on a 6-foot-8 frame, it may not look all that impressive," Cohen said.

Sex can also be great — or challenging.

"[Relationship expert] Betty Dodson noted that the Kama Sutra was created by small Yogi people. There are a lot of positions in there no one should be doing, let alone tall people. There's certain positions that work well if you're tall, and certain ones you can't do."

Are the mentally disabled off-limits to ask out?

They asked:

I was at work when a hot chick walked in with her parents. She was outgoing, positive, a beam of sunshine, and obviously mentally handicapped. I wonder: would it be ethical to date the mentally challenged?

Guy, 45, Boise, Idaho

You said::

Are you serious? Why would any man not developmentally disabled want to date a woman who is? People who seek others with a disadvantage (financial, mental, etc.) often have unresolved issues. It is unhealthy and dysfunctional.

S.D., 38, female, Tampa

Thanks for your response. When I was younger, I ... was dating a girl with a degree, issues and an awful attitude. So I think it fair to ask: a happy, well-adjusted person but not intelligent, or a neurotic, unhappy person with a Ph.D. and boatload of issues? I think the answer is clear. Do you automatically see dating any handicapped person as inherently unethical or sick? Isn't it possible these people have something to offer?

Guy, 45, Boise, Idaho

If you're a 45-year-old asking this question, you're probably neither smart nor happy. I wonder how she would cope with it.

Celeron, 19, male, Maplewood, N.J.

What if she was hot and had a great personality? Look at Jessica Simpson, she obviously needs adult supervision to make it through a day.

Guy, 45, Boise, Idaho

We found:

Is it ever OK to date the mentally disabled? Jonathan Mooney says the answer is a "big, fat yes."

"Individuals with these differences should be treated as any other human being," said Mooney, who despite severe learning disabilities graduated with honors from Brown University and wrote "The Short Bus: A Journey Beyond Normal."

"They have a right to enter even dysfunctional relationships, and the right to the continuum of human experiences that aren't always positive."

There are parameters, of course, as with any relationship, said Mooney, who is also founder of Project Eye to Eye, a mentoring non-profit for students with learning differences. Those entering such a relationship should have an authentic motivation, and if there's a significant mental functioning difference, should not take advantage of the mentally disabled person. If caretakers are involved, they should see whether the relationship involves two consenting adults, and whether any abuse of power is occurring.

"But that shouldn't be extrapolated to everyone," he said. "Some people with Down syndrome can enter into a consensual relationship, but there are 25-year-olds with the mental age of a 5-year-old."

Don't forget, too, that there are many "intelligences" in human beings, he said, including emotion, humor, kindness, empathy and the capacity for joy in one's life.

"IQ is just the tip of the iceberg," he said. "Immediacy, a lack of mind-games, a beautiful simplicity ... one could argue there's a capacity to have a more authentic relationship with someone who doesn't have a traditional set of intelligences.

"We shouldn't view the disabled through a lens of pity and infantilize them."

If you're really obese, that could be on you

They asked:

How do really obese people get that way? Isn't there a point where one realizes how fat they are?

Kari, 28, Philadelphia

You said::

The same way J.Lo got her butt and my brother got blue eyes: genetics.

Aysha, 27, Ammon, Idaho

With dieting, if your metabolism slows, you can eat a salad and gain weight or a tub of ice cream and gain weight, so why not just eat whatever tastes better?

Leann, 28, Hobart, Ind.

I was married to a very abusive man who accused me of having an affair with every man who said hello to me in public. I packed on over 100 pounds and realized I did it to make myself more unappealing to outsiders.

Rachel, 36, Canada

I'm 5 feet 6 inches and weigh 260 pounds. I used to work out with weights, play tennis and exercise. I injured my back. I'm not blaming my weight on a medical condition, but it did contribute. I continued to eat the same amount, but being sedentary, I gained weight very fast.

Jeanne, 41, Aiken, S.C.

DNA and metabolism has a lot to do with it. I weighed 170 in high school and for my height and build, that would be ideal for now, but because I believed society's crap about fat women, I have lost and gained numerous times and am now unhealthy.

D., 51, female, Fort Worth

I don't think fat people think they aren't fat. Thankfully, my tall, thin boyfriend disagrees with today's standard of ... heroin-chic as the look to be attained.

Sara, 27, Scranton, Penn.

In my case it makes no rational sense.

K., Dallas

We found:

Very large? You're still in charge ... of what got you so large.

That's almost always the case, said Robert A. Rosati, former director of the Rice Diet Program and associate professor emeritus of medicine at Duke University.

Massive weight gain rarely arises from thyroid or other physical problems, said Rosati, whose clinic is in Durham, N.C., was known to some as the Diet Capital of the World and others as "Fat City" or "The Lourdes of Lard."

"It's habit. While you should say, 'I know better than to do this, I could get diabetes or whatever,' when you're doing it, you don't think that. You may know it intellectually, but when you're in the behavior, you're not aware it's bad for you."

For most morbidly obese folks, things have gone way beyond food and into loneliness, boredom, emotional or even childhood issues, said Rosati, co-author of the New York Times bestselling *The Rice Diet Solution*. The more they eat, the less they can do, so the more pounds packed on for the same amount of food eaten.

The easiest solution: Be aware of why you eat, and stay away from the processed junk the food industry puts out to make it harder for us to stop, Rosati said.

"The manufacturers who add sugar, salt and fat in just the right quantities to keep us wanting more are exacerbating things, because it makes us feel better at the time when we eat it."

Step this way: blind people at the crosswalk

They asked:

I've seen blind people waiting at intersections to cross the street, but how do they know when to cross?

Jennifer, Maryville, Tenn.

You said::

When someone goes blind (or is born blind), the other senses attempt to compensate for the lack of information that the eyes supply. For example, a blind person can "feel" a wall before they walk into it. ... A blind person's sense of hearing is more sensitive than the sighted. They listen for cars coming from the directions of the street they're trying to cross. Some intersections have bells that ring when it's safe to cross. Others have seeing-eye dogs that know when to cross.

S.S.R., 49, female, Penn.

They listen to the traffic. When there's none coming from the dangerous directions, cross. A sighted person can see a blind person at the crosswalk and ask, "Can I help you?" The blind person could say, "Yes, may I take your arm and you can lead me across." When assisting a blind person, do not grab their elbow and push them forward. Rather, offer your arm, and let them hold onto it, and walk slightly ahead of them, with you leading.

Laurie, Boston

A lot of cities now have crossing lights with audible cues, and even where these don't exist, there are environmental cues, like a lot of cars stopping, or other people beginning to walk.

A., 40, Kansas City, Mo.

We found:

Sometimes NPR commentator Beth Finke of Chicago, who is blind, is minding her own business, just standing at a crosswalk even though she's got a green light. Folks going by think she's got a loser for a seeing-eye dog.

Ah, but Finke's got a vision.

"I like to wait until I hear the traffic rushing back and forth in front of me stop, and then the traffic that is parallel to me start," said Finke, author of a children's book about seeing-eye dogs called "Hanni and Beth: Safe & Sound" as well as the memoir "Long Time, No See." "That way I know it's a fresh green light, and I have a long time to cross."

Far from being a loser, her dog even practices the Zen-like "intelligent disobedience" — for example, if it sees traffic coming or a huge pothole, it won't budge even if Finke orders it to do so.

Close calls? Once a cabbie pulled in front of Finke but her dog stopped on a dime — Finke petted the "bejesus" out of her after that one — and once an SUV took a left and nearly squashed them both. Her dog pushed her out of the way, and neither was seriously hurt.

"The guy said, 'Sorry, I didn't see the dog.' I thought, what am I, chopped liver?"

You can help, too: Say "hello" to let her know you're there if she needs assistance.

That's better than saying you wish you could take your dog everywhere ("If I were brave enough [I'd say], 'Well, you could gouge your eyes out.' ") and much better than petting or distracting her dog when its harness is on.

What about her other senses?

"[People] think blind people hear better or have an enhanced sense of touch. I often wonder, is there an assumption people who are deaf can 'see' better?"

Does it take all kinds to be depressed?

They asked:

I read Phillip Milano's book "I Can't Believe You Asked That!" and was especially intrigued by the entry on depression by 14-year-old Katie. I was wondering, who else suffers from depression?

David, Los Angeles

Note to readers: Katie posted a message to our site, Yforum.com, some time back, alluding to possible plans for suicide. She was in our previous book. We advised local authorities, who talked with her and her parents.

You said::

I do, as does everyone in my family. It's insidious and can ruin your life. Talk therapy is supposed to be best. Medications can keep you functioning, and I disagree with those who criticize people for using them.

Margaret, 52, Belmont, Calif.

I read the book, too, and was also intrigued by that entry. I suffer from depression, though it is not as bad as it was. I was put into therapy and given medication after my mom found a journal entry that expressed my plans for suicide. When not depressed, I am upbeat, friendly and comical. When I don't know how to feel, depression is my default.

A.E., female, Ohio

I did, because I thought the world would hate me for being gay. I'm still not sure how people will react, but I am no longer suicidal.

Jacob, 17, Minnesota

Tens of millions suffer from depression in the U.S. Prozac is one of the most prescribed drugs. I've been on medication for decades. It's not an exact science ... but it's worth it when you find the right combination of meds. If you can't afford certain meds, some drug companies have special programs for low-income patients.

S., 50, female, St. Louis

We found:

Anyone can get depressed, but women are twice as likely to be diagnosed as men, said Richard O'Connor, a psychotherapist and author of "Undoing Depression." Men are four times as likely to commit suicide, he said.

"Men tend not to mess around and choose lethal means, whereas women often survive," said O'Connor, whose mother committed suicide.

Nearly 7 percent of Americans will experience a major depression in their lifetime, but add in subtler forms and it can affect up to 25 percent, he said.

Often, O'Connor's patients don't complain of depression but of all the problems in their lives — bad marriage, work stress, alcohol, etc. But undiagnosed depression, which causes lethargy, a sense of hopelessness and more, may have led to the troubles in the first place.

"Everybody has emotionally rough times, but people prone to depression have a special reaction to tough news, and it starts a vicious circle," he said.

Medication can help, but therapy and reaching out to friends and loved ones can offer more long-term solutions.

"I hear lots of sad stories from my post office clerk, for example," O'Connor said. "She's always cheerful, but feels lonely and desperate inside. Lots of people pass things off. It doesn't do your depression any good."

Will a wheelchair user take it sitting down when you crouch?

They asked:

I recently met a man in a wheelchair. After I left, I wondered if I had been impolite by talking to him from a higher position. Would it be better if I had crouched alongside him?

Richard, 54, Los Angeles

You said::

There is no need to crouch as if stooping to speak to a child. Just because someone is in a wheelchair does not mean they are stupid — I have a 160 IQ.

Susan, 37, have lupus, Chicago

If you're going to talk for a while, about serious things, maybe find somewhere to sit where you're comfortable, too. If it's a quick "hey what's up" or short chat, then really no need.

Kimberley, 40, double above-knee amputee, Whitefish, Mont.

I'm sure the man you were talking to realizes his situation and accepts that just about everybody he talks to is taller than he is. Does an NBA player crouch down when he speaks to somebody shorter than he is? The only reasons I can think of to crouch is if it's a child, or some sort of a king who will have you beheaded if you don't.

Ron, 60, Stockton, Calif.

I would've asked him if he'd be more comfortable with you sitting. My neck hurts when I've been looking up at someone while we converse.

D., 51, morbidly obese female, Fort Worth

During the months I spent in a wheelchair, I would have appreciated someone crouching when we spoke at length, because my neck would get sore if I had to look up for long.

Kathy, Calgary

We found:

At first we thought we'd just get comments from your average person who hangs out in a wheelchair and stuff.

Then we found out about this guy who goes upside-down in his. So we rolled with him.

Aaron Fotheringham of Las Vegas has spina bifida and uses a wheelchair. Does that stop him from doing the insane things any red-blooded teen might do? Guess.

Fotheringham, an Extreme wheelchair athlete who's been on the Nitro Circus Live tour, is the first person to nail a backflip, double-backflip and frontflip in a wheelchair.

So, what does he say about people who crouch down?

"I do get upset. It's like stooping to my level. It makes it look like, 'oh, the little kid.' "

Adults do it the most.

"They think they want to make eye contact . . . I know they're not purposely being mean, but it's just insulting."

Not as bad as an able-bodied person taking the handicapped bathroom stall, though.

"That's my biggest pet peeve. Sometimes to make them look bad, I'll get up and use the regular stall and leave my wheelchair outside. They're like 'Oh . . . ' They'll come out and make eye contact and then lower their head and leave.

"And I'm like 'Yeah, you should be ashamed!' "

There once was a (mentally disabled) crooked-teethed man...

They asked:

Is it true that more people with mental disabilities have oversized and crooked teeth?

D.M.V., 35

You said::

I've never heard that. That's interesting. A good deal of this population would be eligible for Medicaid coverage, which does not cover (for the most part) any dental work. My brother is mentally challenged and has had several teeth pulled due to major bone loss in his jaw. My parents paid for his teeth implants out of pocket because, according to my mother, he only has so much going for him, and it would be devastating if he didn't even have all of his teeth.

Annie, 51, Lawrenceville, Ga.

There are two reasons for your observation. First, people with mental disabilities are less likely to realize the value of good dental hygiene . . . and as a result, [their teeth] end up crooked. Second, many people with mental disabilities actually have good teeth, good grooming habits, etc. And thus, they are less likely to be recognized as being "different." You could have passed 10 mentally challenged people today on the street, all with good teeth, and never knew they were handicapped.

Kortni, Denver

We found:

First, to be clear: In most states, if you're under 21 and eligible, Medicaid will cover basic dentistry and some orthodontic work. The latter is generally reserved for a medical necessity, such as pretty severe malocclusions (for us non-dental experts, that's when teeth don't meet properly when you bite down).

If you're 21 or older, dental coverage gets dicier, depending on the state.

The late Carlton Horbelt, past president of the Special Care Dentistry Association (www.scdonline.org), talked with us before his death. He looked into a lot of the mouths of the intellectually disabled for more than two decades.

"(Crooked teeth) is a fairly common finding with developmental syndromes," he said. "It's not necessarily just people with intellectual disabilities, but any genetic syndrome that produces physical abnormalities or intellectual disabilities."

With conditions such as Down, Apert or Crouzon syndromes, for example, there can be oral abnormalities — such as a delay in the eruption of teeth, spacing problems or teeth coming in in the wrong order — that can result in crooked teeth, he said.

The danger often is not lack of treatment, but too much of it, Horbelt said.

"There can be a tendency for a private office to overtreat. That's not a criticism, because they want to offer the best care possible."

The problem is that corrective bridgework, dentures or partials may not be advisable if the patient can't maintain them, he told us. Or, in the case of cerebral palsy (in which the person may fall a lot), fixed bridgework in the mouth can dislodge and become a choking hazard.

"In the end you have to stand back and say, what can the person tolerate? That's the difference: You want to offer the very best dentistry that they can tolerate."

Short people got no reason to be upset?

They asked:

Do shorter people ever get upset about how short they are, or are they OK with it? Do they ever get frustrated with not being able to reach certain things, or from getting weird looks?

R. Baldwin, Mount Carmel, Tenn.

You said::

I have a close friend who is 4 feet 6 inches, and yes, she gets weird looks and gets a little irritated at the height of certain things (such as ATMs), but all in all she's fine with her height. Usually it's other people who seem to have a problem with it.

M.G., 34, female, Jacksonville

I used to be self-conscious about being short (I'm 5 feet 2 inches) but am just fine with it now. I don't care for people who comment on my stature or mention how difficult it must be. I am who I am.

A.C., 24, female, Iowa

We found:

We were at the height of frustration because apparently short people had, no reason, short people had, no reason . . . to get back to us on this one.

It wasn't like we were asking them to get on a soapbox or anything. Just tell us what it's like to not have elevation. To exist in a non-alpine-like state. For altitudinous to not describe you. To be lank-less.

Finally, a football player and a former politician rose to the challenge.

First there's 5-foot-7-inch Maurice Jones-Drew, the former NFL running back who's plowed over, through and by more than a few linebackers.

Does it bug him being shorter?

"My whole thing is, I'm a realist. I can't change my height," said "M.J.D." now an NFL Network analyst. "If I can't reach something, I'll get a ladder. Otherwise, I won't be trying to grab it."

His philosophy?

"My grandpa said once you look for the negative side, or let people give you excuses, then you're showing a sign of weakness."

His response to ribbing as a kid?

"You fight through things by showing a sign of strength. I'd say [about someone who teased him], 'I don't have to be as big as him.' Then you start to believe in it. To kids today I would say, one thing no one else can measure is your mind and your heart. And you can do anything with those two things."

Then there's 5-foot-6-inch former Jacksonville Mayor John Peyton, who responded by e-mail. Does it bug him being shorter?

"I think if you're comfortable with yourself, other people are comfortable with you, too — so my lack of tallness hasn't been a problem for me anywhere but the basketball court!"

His philosophy?

"I view my height as a distinguishing characteristic rather than an impediment. It's also a great icebreaker. I [recently] had to introduce [former Jacksonville Jaguars NFL tackle] Tony Boselli at a press conference. Standing next to this guy, who I believe is at least 10 feet tall, I made a comment about him being twice my size . . . everybody laughed, and we got the event off to a good start."

His response to ribbing as a kid?

"I took some teasing in my teenage years, but I chalk that up to character development — it's never a bad thing to develop a little humility."

Is sex only a little sexy for someone sightless?

They asked:

With all the trials and tribulations blind people must contend with, I wonder how, well, "lust" is handled. A sighted person can look upon a beautiful woman or handsome man and feel pleasure. Is the blind person reduced to feelings of extreme frustration that only lovemaking can relieve, or is fantasy and imagination able to lessen the annoying "itch" nearly all of us experience?

John, 41, Boston

You said::

I have a close friend who's been blind since birth. He does fantasize, thinking of past sexual experiences, sounds and sensations (he has much to draw upon). He does not miss what he never had.

Cassandra, 36, Chicago

I don't think I am reduced to frustration because I can't look at a man. There is so much more to the sexiness of a person than how they look. If a man is charming in his thoughts and words, I can be attracted to him. Also, masculine colognes mixed with the natural body scent can be arousing. Needless to say, tactile and aural sensations are the best. A pleasing voice and soft touches are wonderful. I don't feel I am deprived of a person's beauty. Fantasy and imagination work for the blind just as for the sighted. The fantasies may be of a different nature, though.

Meri C., 22, blind, Italy

We found:

Lynn Manning has seen lust from both sides of the lens: sighted and unsighted.

The Los Angeles playwright and actor even discusses the topic in a play he's completing titled "In the Absence of Light."

"In it, a character speaks of drinking a woman in with his eyes, and his blind friend wishes he could," said Manning, who lost his sight to a gunshot at age 23.

In his play "Object Lesson," a blind character who was into porn movies before losing his sight tries to get his new girlfriend to "describe the action" happening on-screen.

"She has an aversion initially, but . . . well, it gets very funny."

His point, he said: Other senses must do the work of fulfilling one's sexual needs.

"The fantasy realm that exists has to move from being visually stimulating to [things such as] the sound of a woman passing by, or of her shoes, or her pantyhose, or her whistling, or her hand on your shoulder, or the tug of the weight of her breast on her bra strap, or the smell of her perfume and hairspray . . ."

We see.

As one can guess, things often must be more up-close and personal to fully resonate.

"You can't gaze at the mountain in the distance; we have to be on the mountain," he said.

Does he miss his sight as it relates to sex?

"You can suffer some drop-off and frustration. For example, say your partner is dressed sexy . . . you can't appreciate that from afar. Or slinky dancing and all of those come-hither poses, it no longer exists."

But, you cope, and you adapt.

"You develop other ways of observing, of piecing together the world around you. . . . All of it provides much fuel for fantasy, much fuel for inspiration."

Why would anyone call another person a 'retard'?

They asked:

Why do people call someone with a disability a retard?

Jessica, West Monroe, N.Y.

You said::

It is derived from "mental retardation," which was thought to be less stigmatizing than "mentally subnormal." It implies that some people are slow or permanently delayed in their intellectual development. It has been used to justify treating them as children for the rest of their lives.

Chris, London

People fear what they do not understand, which in a way is very sad. There are people hindered by a disability . . . but are they really? Many reach beyond their handicaps and make the most of their lives. It's all in how you desire to live. It doesn't take any talent to sit in a corner and suck your thumb. What does take talent is to live your life to the fullest. Think about it: Who is the real retard? Someone who never accesses their talent, or someone who strives, no matter the obstacles? Next time you see someone who is physically (or mentally) challenged, think: Would you be able to cope as they have?

Lindsay, 49, San Antonio

In French, "retard" means late. I'm not sure but maybe that has something to do with the way a lot of people call those with disabilities slow?

Shelly, 16, Little Rock, Ark.

We found:

Well, actually, according to Google, in French, "retard" means delay and "tard" means late.

The pejorative "retard" does, of course, come from the diagnostic condition of mental retardation, which the American Association on Intellectual and Developmental Disabilities (AAIDD) defines as a disability originating before age 18 "characterized by significant limitations both in intellectual functioning and in adaptive behavior as expressed in conceptual, social and practical adaptive skills."

As a matter of fact, until not too long ago, AAIDD was known as the American Association on Mental Retardation. It decided to move away from that name because "mental retardation" itself had become a stigmatizing term and was disliked by those with disabilities and their families, said former Executive Director Doreen Croser.

That name, however, was at least better than its original moniker when founded in 1876: The Association of Medical Officers of American Institutions for Idiotic and Feeble-Minded Persons. Whoa.

To use "retard" to describe someone is to take on the attitude that "anyone different is [to be] the victim of ridicule and abuse," she said.

"In certain segments it's OK to be mean and hateful. The media doesn't help. There are lots of morning talk show folks who need to be corrected routinely, calling people retards."

As nasty words fall out of favor, others always seem to rush in to fill the void because, she said, "hate is in, unfortunately."

"Now, they use the phrase 'developmental disability' in school, so kids on the playground are calling kids 'developmentals.' "

Listen up hearing people, and see how your treat the deaf

They asked:

Why do hearing people treat us deafies like we are not fit for their society? They act like they want nothing to do with us. They get aggravated with us. Or they attempt to talk louder, slower and with wider mouth movement. What gives?

Kimberly, 48, deaf, Jacksonville

You said::

How are we supposed to talk to you if you can't hear, and we don't know sign language? It's true a lot of it has to do with ignorance, but many people don't do it to offend — we just haven't been taught the proper way to speak to a deaf person.

Reign, 19, female, Illinois

Talking louder, slower or with wider mouth movements is not an act of contempt. It's an attempt to connect with you. Hearing people . . . are doing the best they can think of, even though on the receiving end it is a pain. If you are feeling up to it, you can educate the hearing person on how you would prefer to be communicated with.

Laurie B., Boston

If it makes you feel any better, these jerks most likely behave the same way toward people who don't speak English.

A., 39, Missouri

We found:

Hearing-impaired comedian Kathy Buckley said something funny to us.

"I can't hear anything at high frequency, like birds. But if you fart, I'm right on it."

To Buckley, an inspirational speaker and author of "If You Could Hear What I See," it's not about treating deaf people poorly, it's about people being anxious communicating.

"I do it myself: Say a person is speaking Japanese and I need to talk with them — I'll automatically raise my voice, because I'm having a discomfort with communication. There's a frustration when we can't communicate. A lot of people will avoid it because they are not comfortable or patient."

Deaf people ought to let hearing people know what they need, though, she said.

"Write it, sign it, mime it, sing it, dance it, whatever it is," she said. "You're only treated the way you treat people. You can't be angry at people's ignorance. If you're not willing to take time to teach, you are just as ignorant as them. No one is here to kiss anybody's butt."

Still, it wouldn't hurt for hearing people to learn more about what it's like to be deaf.

"What I hate is if I'm with you and someone says something to you and you laugh, and I say, 'What did they say?' and you say, 'Oh, I'll tell you later.' Well, I know I'll never hear it, so I just got cut out of the loop."

And hearing people, LISTEN UP: Have you seen how you look lately?

"We [deaf people] really see facial expressions. People don't realize how intense they look," Buckley said. "So put a nice look on. It's common courtesy."

Perhaps don't tremble over those tremors

They asked:

My nerves tighten from cerebral hypoxia. It's not noticeable except a slight trembling of my hands. I can't lift a martini glass without spilling it. I'm very attractive but have always felt embarrassed and haven't dated. How will I meet a nice guy?

Anna, 27, Staten Island, N.Y.

You said::

Most guys I know would love a drink spilled on them by a beautiful woman, if for no other reason than it is an "in" to a conversation.

Doug G., 25, Lisle, Ill.

If the guy is worth your time, he won't mind. He probably won't notice. Love is blind!

Andy, 30, Columbus, Ohio

Oh my God, are we sisters? I have the same thing. Have you spoken to your doctor? Tell him your condition affects your social life.

Brandy, 26, Salina, Kan.

My hands have shaken all my life. Be yourself and you'll meet guys . . . or, you could switch from martinis to bottled beer.

Sean, 23, Denver

Your nice guy isn't at a bar unless you want to be . . . told he will be there for you as he slips out the window with bedsheets and a broken-down Buick Skylark. My suggestion: Go to the bars to let your hair down, enjoy your work and have fun.

Mike, 27, Chicago

My advice: Think of those who have it worse than you, get yourself out there . . . and just ask for a straw.

Cindy, 30, Appleton, Wis.

No matter what is different, someone will ridicule. The trick is not caring about the jerks and concentrating on the nice people.

Bill, 49, Dry Ridge, Ky.

We found:

Anna may fall in the broad category of people with cerebral palsy: those who had something happen to their brain before age 2 who have motor problems such as spasticity or trembling, says Mindy Aisen, chief of neurorehabilitation at the University of Southern California and former executive director of the United Cerebral Palsy Research and Educational Foundation.

Anna also falls in the broad category of people with tremor: everybody.

"We all have it, but in most cases it's not obvious. It can be brought out with coffee or anxiety. For people with CP, it's just an inability to turn it off."

Someone with a more noticeable tremor should still "get out and mix," Aisen said. "Some young people want to disguise it. You must look others right in the face and say, 'I am what I am, and I am important, too.' "

If anxiety worsens the problem, medications can help, so Anna might want to see a neurologist, Aisen added.

Also, there's nothing wrong with a little practice and planning before social situations.

"For example, probably soup isn't the best choice at a restaurant. You might try finger foods like a hamburger and fries. You can also plan out where you will be going, and what obstacles there will be to overcome. You can practice saying what you will order, looking people in the eye, relaxing. It's about building up your confidence."

Look closer, deaf are all around in the work force

They asked:

What do deaf people do to earn a living? I rarely see deaf people in my corporate role, in retail or service industry roles, or anywhere else.

Laura, 48, Jacksonville

You said::

OK, now that I have calmed down . . . I have many friends who are deaf. My ophthalmologist is deaf. They work for the federal government. They are computer technicians, own their own businesses, are artists, work in banks. They work at Wal-Mart and Publix. My boyfriend was the first deaf member of the carpenters union in Connecticut. Most of all, they are proud of their culture, which starts with a capital "D"!

Carol, 52, Florida

I've had several co-workers who were deaf and could read lips and speak so well you wouldn't have known they were deaf until they told you. And for those who can't, I know here on the First Coast there is the Florida School for the Deaf and the Blind. I'm sure for those people, being a teacher at a specialty school for deaf children or something along those lines is an option.

Cassy, 22, Jacksonville

You can find deaf people working in jobs such as data entry, as cashiers in stores and also as educators, readers to the blind, etc.

Michele D., 38, Jacksonville

We found:

Listen, and listen good, says Karen Black, former spokeswoman for the National Technical Institute for the Deaf at Rochester Institute of Technology:

Deaf . . . people . . . work!

"There are deaf engineers. IT specialists. Chemists. There are deaf people in the courtroom, operating room, boardroom. In fact, there are so many more higher-educated deaf workers in recent years that it's caused a shortage of higher-educated interpreters."

According to a study in the Journal of the American Academy of Audiology, 58 percent of deaf people in the 18 to 44 age bracket are employed, compared to 82 percent of the general population in that age range, while 46 percent of deaf people ages 45 to 64 are working, compared to 73 percent of the general population that age.

Deaf people often tend to cluster in cities and companies that are most open to them, Black noted. For example, at nearly 13 percent, the Rochester, N.Y., metro area has the largest deaf population per capita in the U.S., according to a New York Times article. Nationally, employers such as Raytheon and Citigroup have attracted large numbers of deaf employees, often using NTID as a resource.

"With excellent lip-reading, hearing aids, cochlear implants or hair that covers the ears, you may not even know a deaf or hearing-impaired person is working with you," Black said.

"I know at first I was intimidated and felt unable to communicate with deaf people, so I avoided them. But people with hearing loss are the most patient, kind people. They just want to communicate. They don't want to be isolated in the workplace. So please make the effort."

Please, no cracks about this tongue condition

They asked:

I've noticed that some people have cracks on their tongues. Why is this?

Walter S., 50, Houston

You said::

I believe I read that one reason is a deficiency of a certain B vitamin.

Laurie B., 55, Boston

I have such a tongue. It causes weird patches and sometime fissures as a result of the papillae wearing off. It is exacerbated by spicy and acidic foods or drinks.

Tracy, 27, Dallas

My dad has cracks on his tongue, and he was told it was caused by his mouth being overly dry. The condition may also have a genetic component: I also have cracks, although not as bad as his.

Daniel, 26, Colorado Springs, Colo.

We found:

Here's a mouthful: benign migratory glossitis. It's an inflammatory condition, more typically known as geographic tongue.

There are actually two separate conditions to be aware of here, says Robert D. Kelsch, an oral pathologist at NorthShore LIj Health System in New Hyde Park, N.Y.

One is "fissured" or "cracked" tongue, which can go hand-in-hand with geographic tongue. Beyond cracks, the latter can lead to red patches on the top, sides and underside of the tongue, with surrounding patches of white borders that are irregular-shaped.

Sounds like . . . a map. Which is where it gets its name.

It can happen in about 20 percent of adults, likely has a hereditary cause though a specific cause is unknown, has no demographic disposition and usually goes away in about seven to 10 days, Kelsch said.

"It has nothing to do with diet or not eating or eating certain foods or vitamin deficiencies or infection or cancer," he said.

However, that doesn't mean if you see something nasty in the mirror when you stick out your tongue that you should just blow it off.

"One of the high-risk sites for oral cancer is the tongue, and it can present as red and white patches, too. Since there can be some overlap in clinical appearance between geographic tongue and oral cancer, it would be a good idea to have it looked at."

Assuming it's geographic tongue, the most common thing to do is just wait for it to go away, though in some more severe cases, a topical steroid can be prescribed, Kelsch said.

And, if acidic foods like tomato juice or vinegar increase the burning sensations of the affliction, then stay away from them during the outbreak.

"Really, the most bothersome thing is not knowing what it is," he said. "Many patients have seen other specialists, some of whom may assume this is some kind of pre-cancerous or fungal or viral infection, and they get put on all sorts of meds, have biopsies done and it doesn't resolve it. By the time they see me, they're very anxious and think it's some more serious disease that's incurable."

Those missing limbs aren't missing out on suitors

They asked:

I am an amputee and on crutches all the time. Would that really keep someone from asking me out?

Samantha, 21, Seattle

You said::

I would certainly be curious about the stump. It's not something you normally see. The thought doesn't gross me out, but it is unusual. After I got over it, I think I would be OK with it.

Chris, 34, Va.

If it keeps someone from dating you, he's not worth it. Don't turn your nose up, however, at a man who actually prefers you as you are. They are not all bad. There is a cover for every pot. Even one missing a handle.

Bob C., 53, Minn.

When is the next flight to Seattle?

Paul, Miami Beach

If I were under 30 I would be wanting to date you. Women missing a leg are as attractive to me as women with large, inviting breasts are to most guys.

Kent, 58, Australia

I had a relationship with an arm amputee. Anna was a clever, handsome, sensitive, charming girl, so I really didn't think about her empty sleeve and her stump. I have never met such an interesting (and sexy) female.

Goran, 29, Yugoslavia

It wouldn't stop me from asking you out, but it's not why I would ask you out, either. It'll keep some people from asking you out, but they probably aren't the people you'd want to spend quality time with. God knows life is short enough without wasting our quality time on the wrong people.

Peter, New York

We found:

Smile, Samantha. With the right attitude you'll soon be using your crutch as a stick to beat suitors off, says Kimberley Barreda (unlimbited.com), a speaker, writer and double above-the-knee amputee who runs a Web site that connects disabled people at amputeegoddess.com.

"Uh, have you seen me? There's no such thing as a gay guy around me. What I tell some girls who think I can't hold my own in a bar is hey, I'm memorable and spectacular and everyone will remember me — you on the other hand are average and unremarkable."

A little feisty, are we?

"I'm tired of guys who assume I'm not already busy. And I get angry when people say 'You're kind of cute for a girl in a wheelchair.' I say, 'You're kind of cute for an idiot.' "

Guys who don't like amputees may wrongly assume they are asexual, needy or even mentally disabled. Or, Barreda says, such men are often young and unsophisticated when it comes to notions of physical beauty. Others are too insecure to lead the way among their peers.

Men attracted to amputees from the get-go — often called "devotees" — are no worse than men with a penchant for blondes or redheads, she adds.

"Those who say it's wrong or is a fetish, to me that implies there is something wrong with the person on the receiving end of such interest. It's not a fetish if it isn't causing a serious hardship in your day-to-day life."

49

Don't sneeze at someone's food allergy

They asked:

My brother doesn't believe my 3-year-old has a peanut allergy. At a recent dinner at his home, every dish but one had nuts in it. He has also made jokes that if my daughter's not good, he'll hold her down and feed her peanut butter. What is his problem?

C. Fox, 39, Santa Clara, Calif.

You said::

This allergy seemed to come out of nowhere a few years back. All of a sudden, folks were being ordered not to send their kids to school with peanut butter sandwiches, all because a tiny yet vocal and litigious minority started making these demands. I know it's a legit allergy, but to a lot of people, it seems like the creation of shrill hypochondriacs. Your brother thinks you're a wacko.

Roger, 45, Los Angeles

One day my parents brought home a dog I turned out to be allergic to. I told them the dog was making me wheeze. They said I would just have to stay away from him. I'm now 30 miles away. Some people don't take allergies seriously.

Me, 25, female, New York

I'd avoid this sicko like the plague.

Dwanny, 51, female, Fort Worth

Unfortunately, food-specific allergies became part of the zeitgeist about the same time as "Environmental Allergies," which are utter horseshit. As a result, a lot of people can't bring themselves to believe someone could be allergic to one food, or one group of foods.

Ann, 37, Kansas City, Mo.

We found:

You feel a tingling on the lips. Your tongue swells. Your chest and throat linings become inflamed as you gasp for air. Your blood pressure plummets and your bronchia constrict. One by one, your vital organs begin to shut down. Then you die.

While this can happen to virtually anyone watching any of the hosts on CBS' "The Talk" interview anyone, it can also occur when people allergic to peanuts accidentally ingest them.

Six percent of the United States' 50 million allergy sufferers are mainly allergic to food or drugs, and each year more than 200 people die from food allergies, says Mike Tringale of the Asthma and Allergy Foundation of America. Food allergies also account for 30,000 emergency room visits a year.

Most people who think food allergies are a sham are uninformed, Tringale said. AAFA surveys reveal that fewer than 20 percent of the public — and only 27 percent of allergy sufferers — realize allergies are an inherited disease of the immune system.

"Allergies are the Rodney Dangerfield of diseases: They get no respect."

But why have food allergies more than doubled the past 25 years? One theory: It's occurring mostly in developed countries, so kids may be growing up in an overly hygienic environment, and their bodies overreact because they haven't adapted to allergens, Tringale said. Or, it could be pure math; as more people with food allergies intermarry, they produce more offspring with food allergies.

And about sado-uncle from Santa Clara:

"It's ignorance or malice on his part," Tringale said. "He needs to be educated. Or kept away before he causes the death of his niece."

If they stutter, let them utter with no interruption

They asked:

How do others feel about someone who stutters badly and is trying to make a statement or ask a question while taking up your time? Should you interrupt and answer?

Shana B., Miami

You said::

As a stutterer as a child, you should give the stutterer respect enough to finish what he or she is trying to say. If you interrupt them, you may get hit, smacked or kicked.

Bedo, 48, male, Straw Plains, Tenn.

It doesn't bother me when people finish my thoughts if they are nice about it. I do get offended by the "you are wasting my time, you buffoon" attitude I sometimes receive. If you approach it the same way you would a person who was "looking for the right word," you should come across all right.

Kæreste, 22, female, Jacksonville

I simply look at them gently while thinking out a shopping list, and wait till they finish — they haven't the foggiest that you were thinking about what to make for dinner, or how great your husband was in bed last night. Plus, they greatly appreciate your patience.

N.D., 40, female, Michigan

If you can't spare an extra 30 seconds to spare someone's feelings, then don't interact with anyone who is different from you.

Kate, Newport, R.I.

I prefer it if people finish a sentence for me if I can't. For whatever reason, if I get caught on a word, I can immediately say it right if someone else says it first.

Kris, 24, male, Williamsburg, Va.

We found:

James Earl Jones. Julia Roberts. Maya Angelou. Vice President Joe Biden. Ron Harper. John Updike. Bo Jackson. Carly Simon. Andrew Lloyd Webber. Greg Louganis. John Stossel.

We talked with none of them. However, they all at one time or another had stuttering problems, which they mostly overcame to accomplish amazing things. (Go ahead, try to imagine being an Olympic diver and a stutterer at the same time. See? Impossible.)

What would seem a no-brainer — we hear it's rude to interrupt anyone — may not always be, says Kenneth O. St. Louis, co-founder of the International Fluency Association and a top researcher on stuttering.

"There are a few instances where stutterers like it when someone fills in their words, especially in severe cases where they have given up on their own ability," said St. Louis, a mostly recovered stutterer himself and a professor of speech-language pathology at West Virginia University. "Usually, though, after some speech therapy and guidance on self-esteem, most don't want someone filling in their words."

In fact, a survey of public attitudes on stuttering that St. Louis shepherded found that most people understand they should essentially ignore the speech impediment and wait for the person to finish.

"Filling in words is often taken by a person as they can't do it themselves — assuming you even can fill in their words. There are lots of instances where someone fills in something a person has no intention of saying. I remember a person who was trying to say 'I,' and the other person kept pointing to his eye. So it often just doesn't help."

What's it like to dream if you don't see?

They asked:

Do folks who have been blind since birth have dreams?

R.W.K., 62, male, Jacksonville

You said::

One of my relatives is blind, and I've read many times that those who are blind from birth dream mostly in other senses, most notably sound and smell. Because most of them have only very little perception in light, I would assume they don't really dream in sight at all.

Rick, Los Alamos, N.M.

I lost my eyesight when I was 6 months old, but for the most part, I don't remember it. Blind people see things in their mind just as anyone else does. It may not look the same as what "seeing people" see, but I still see it — a tree, a car or myself. And when I dream, that is no exception. So the color red to you may be different than my color red, but it's red to me.

Jordan, 19, blind male, Springfield, Mo.

I went blind at 23, and I still dream the same way I did before losing my sight: with "pictures." I actually see what I am dreaming about — the way I remember things looking, and much the same way I dreamed before losing my sight. I am not sure if this would be the same as someone who is blind from birth, as they don't really know what things look like because they have never seen the items. I make a concentrated effort not to forget the sight of things I hold dearest to me, such as the face of my little boy, and the way the snow looks on a crisp December morning.

Samantha, 27, blind female, Brandon, Canada

We found:

To sum up nearly a century's worth of detailed studies on whether blind people have visual imagery in their dreams:

Blind after age 7: Likely. Blind between 5-7: Possible. Blind between 0-5: Seldom. Blind since birth: In your dreams.

This is not to say that people blind from birth don't dream as imaginatively as sighted people. For example, a major study by the universities of Hartford, California and Connecticut of 15 blind adults found that subjects blind from birth used a high percentage of taste, smell and touch sensations to describe the imagery in their dreams: They "felt" the warmth of the sun, texture of a coat or edge of a knife; "smelled" fire, tobacco, aftershave lotion or fresh air; and "tasted" a cigar, cup of coffee or an orange.

"The imagery and sensations in the dreams of the blind are generally continuous with the senses they use in their waking lives," the researchers noted.

As National Federation of the Blind spokeswoman Pat Maurer put it, what is experienced in a dream varies with each blind person.

"Maybe they wouldn't picture a chair in the same way a sighted person would, but everyone has been in a chair before, so they have some notion of what it feels like," she said. "And based on what they believe it looks like, they would base their perception in their dream on that impression."

Maurer, who lost her sight over time after receiving too much oxygen in her incubator as a premature baby, said the images in her own dreams have faded with the decades.

"As a younger person, the pictures were more distinct ... now I still see a picture of a person, for example, but I don't know how close to reality it is."

Are Down kids down with their differences?

They asked:

Do Down syndrome kids realize they have a disability?

Sam, 15, female, St. Charles, Ill.

You said::

I worked for years with people with Down syndrome. I'm sure they know they're different. It depends on how high-functioning they are, how much they really "get." Also, the older they are, the more they realize differences.

Ellen, 44, Mesa, Ariz.

I used to baby-sit for a Down syndrome boy. He was aware he was different because when we would go somewhere and people would stare at him, he would scare them and laugh about it. He didn't let it upset him, and he was only 12 at the time. He had a great sense of humor and did well in school. He understood he was different but didn't let it be a disability for him.

Traci, 27, Jacksonville

I work with a guy who has Down syndrome. Although he can be hard to understand, he isn't dumb. He has a name, and I treat him as an equal. I'm proud to be his friend, and I'm sure he knows he has some obstacles — just like the mentally handicapped know when they're being made fun of. But I admire how they can smile and live their lives to the fullest.

David, 21, Houston

We found:

Research suggests children with Down syndrome become acutely mindful around age 9 or 10 that they don't perform as well as their peers in some areas. However, awareness varies with the individual, said Dr. Dennis McGuire of the Global Down Syndrome Foundation in Denver, Colo.

"Most have a good sense they are different," said McGuire, who has counseled upward of 3,000 people with Down syndrome. "They are aware of people's responses [and] if people stare or treat them differently."

A majority of those with Down syndrome "are doing fine" with their situation, he said, but about 10 percent have "acceptance issues" and can isolate themselves.

"Those folks have some major problems because ... they don't accept others with Down syndrome, yet they aren't as accepted themselves by the general population."

Challenges can arise for children in strict "inclusive" or "mainstreaming" programs who lack access to others with Down syndrome, McGuire said.

"You have to have some relationships with your peers because they are the ones you connect to who are going through the same developmental stuff you are. A lot of these folks ... when the other kids without Down syndrome go on to college, or go out on dates, the kids with Down syndrome are left behind."

Most, however, are like David Jonaitis of Wilmette, Ill.

"I have a good life with having Down syndrome," said Jonaitis, who works as a grocery bagger and retail clerk. "I like to dance, I like to play sports and go to movies. People are very nice to me."

What should others know about him?

"Some people just need encouragement and honesty, so be nice to one another, and be yourself and just be cool. Be a friend. Be a compassionate person."

Invisible and overweight can bring you down

They asked::

My weight has yo-yo'd most of my life. When I'm heavier, men seem to have more of a negative reaction. Is this because of the media presentation of what the ideal woman should look like?

Susan, 45, Flint, Mich.

You said::

The response I get from people has much more to do with my feelings about myself and my self-presentation than my weight. When I feel sexy and good, whether I'm Twiggy or Zaftig makes no difference.

Omphale, 29, female, Minneapolis

If the media would just portray an average woman who is not a Paris Hilton lookalike, maybe everyone would see how beautiful women can be with a little meat on their bones.

Kim M., 21, Swartz Creek, Mich.

Why blame the media? Has it ever occurred to people that the media portrays the ideal woman that way because that's the ideal woman?

Rajah, 22, male, Watertown, Wis.

I generally avoid overweight women as partners. I don't want a woman who isn't healthy or possibly has a ton of self-esteem issues. It's crazy women blame Paris Hilton and men for not accepting them. If you're too heavy, go to the gym and eat better.

John, 22, Springville, N.Y.

What's crazy is how much positive reinforcement people get for losing weight. I dropped about 10 pounds one time because of a health problem and got so many positive comments I was left thinking, "Just how bad did I look before?" and "For Pete's sake, I've been sick and people are applauding me for looking so good?"

Sharon, 25, Fairfax, Va.

We found:

Julie Ridl, founder of "The Skinny Daily Post" at skinnydaily.com, uses blogs to chronicle her experiences before and after shedding 100 pounds, as well as her struggles with Lyme disease. She says people weren't really negative when she was large. Just oblivious.

"I could literally be in a room without being in the room. There's a lack of eye contact, no conversations on the elevator. Now I step on the elevator and there's immediate conversation. In meetings I don't have to fight to be heard."

She says the media do help create stigmas and stereotypes.

"In news reports about how America is getting 'fat,' they'll show images of obese people with their heads 'cut off,' or shoving burgers in their mouths. There are more creative ways of talking about weight."

Meanwhile, a study published in the American Journal of Public Health found that in prime-time TV, overweight female characters were "less likely to be considered attractive or interact with romantic partners," while overweight males were less likely "to talk about dating and more likely to be shown eating."

"It's not just romance issues these stereotypes create," Ridl says. "Try buying a car or house as a fat person. I hear overweight people all the time who experience prejudice. It's heartbreaking."

Do the disabled like it when we try to help?

They asked:

Is it appropriate to hold the door or go out of my way to help an individual in a wheelchair?

Joe M., Sioux Falls, S.D.

You said::

My girlfriend, a wheelchair user, says to wait to be asked if you're a stranger. Spontaneous pushing of a wheelchair is invasive and sometimes very frightening.

Andy B., 27, St. Albans, United Kingdom

It is annoying and rude when people try to do things for me. It's as if they think that just because I am disabled, I am in need of help. I have seen people ask able-bodied people [for help], so why not give the disabled person the same courtesy? Of course, if you and the disabled person are going in at the same time, hold the door open so your toes don't get rolled over.

Luticha, 21, paralyzed, Fairport, N.Y.

I think it's important to remember the Golden Rule in this situation. If you were in a wheelchair, would you want someone to open a door for you? I certainly would. I used to volunteer at a camp for handicapped children and teens, and one of the exercises they had us do was to sit in a wheelchair and try to navigate through normal situations such as opening doors. Let me tell you, it's not easy. It's always better to do the "nice" thing, and if the person misconstrues it, let that be on their head.

Christy, Jacksonville

We found:

If you're going to try and be nice to someone in a wheelchair, don't do what a person did to Ms. Wheelchair America 2005.

"He opened the main door for me to go into a building — I was heading in and he was heading out," said Juliette Rizzo. "The problem was there was a second set of doors inside, but this person didn't offer to open them, so I sat in between until someone came along to open the next set. They looked at me and wondered what I was doing there."

Such goof-ups aside, most people want to do the right thing, and that's good, said Rizzo, who helps coordinate events at the U.S. Department of Education and works out at a boxing gym to boot. They should relax and be themselves, but they should remember that people with disabilities are the best judges of what they can and cannot do.

"I find it respectful when people ask [if she wants help]. I was recently at a huge banquet in Atlanta, and the woman next to me said, 'I am aware you can do a lot of things, but should you need some help, I'm a helpful individual and am happy to do so.' She didn't force herself on me or start to cut my food. She just extended an offer of help to a partner at the table. We want to be treated as independent people."

And, not to go too far off tangent (we are on the subject of helping out), don't dawdle if you have no disability but are using the wheelchair stall in a public restroom, says Brewster Thackeray, consultant to the National Organization on Disability and executive director of The ENDependence Center of Northern Virginia.

"Someone who is disabled may come along and need it."

The O.U.T.L.O.U.D. Method to Dialogue

OPEN UP: This is mostly about opening up to yourself. Why do you want to engage someone? Is it for the right reasons? The answers might help you figure out how to approach another person. A friend once told me the real reason I started Y? wasn't for me to learn more about "Buddhists in Asia or lesbians in San Francisco," but because I wanted to learn something more about myself. He was right. Acknowledging that has helped give me perspective when considering others' answers.

USE YOUR HEAD: Plan for the right question. Not all questions need to be the "wet dogs" variety. Stereotypes and clichés don't work as well as sincere attempts to talk.

TIME IT RIGHT: Create the "O.U.T.L.O.U.D. Moment". Pick your spots for provocative dialogue. Find a genuine opening rather than create a false one. It's often during those down times between all the "vital" discourse that we can most easily find a direct path to someone's point of view. If you spend enough time sitting in the cubicle next to someone of a different culture, chances are there'll come a time — over food, perhaps, or during a power outage — when the topic you've been dying to broach will wend its way naturally into the discussion.

LOCK IN ON THE TARGET: Keeping things simple can give the best chance for getting another's trust and a meaningful reply. Some of the best questions at Y?, those that prompt the most telling answers, are also often the easiest to digest. Remember, it's not about winning your point. It's what comes from the heart that counts most — and captures people's interest. Talking from the heart also means easing into things by letting someone know *why* it would help you to learn the answer to your question before you ask it.

OWN UP TO ASSUMPTIONS: One of the most refreshing and repetitive surprises of the Y? project is the difficulty in predicting how a person will respond to a question. Blacks do not think in lockstep. Nor do whites. Nor Christians or Muslims, Nor gays or straights. Be receptive to another's ideas. Wipe the slate clean and listen to the content of the message, not the color or culture of the messenger.

UNLOAD YOUR EXPECTATIONS: Many of us are thinner-skinned than we'll admit. When we get hit with an answer or comment we hadn't anticipated, our emotions can often get caught off-balance, and our egos get bruised. The solution: Expect the unexpected. You'll never be blindsided or taken aback by information that doesn't gibe with your worldview.

DIGEST THE DIALOGUE: Learning about others doesn't stop when the talking's over. Assess what you're told and how it fits with or departs from your perspectives. Recap your discussion with a third party to distill the most relevant information into its most meaningful points.

ABOUT THE AUTHOR

Phillip J. Milano is the founder of Y? The National Forum on People's Differences, the acclaimed cross-cultural dialogue project that encourages people to ask unflinching, politically incorrect questions about our differences.

Since its creation in 1998, Phillip's web site, YForum.com, has attracted millions of visitors and thousands of questions and answers. He has been featured on CBS, CNN, BET and the BBC, and in numerous newspapers, including The Washington Post, New York Times and USA Today.

He is the author of the Perigee book "I Can't Believe You Asked That!" as well as writer of the pioneering newspaper column/blog "Dare to Ask."

Mr. Milano is a 25-year newspaper veteran. He received his Master of Business Administration from Northern Illinois University and his Bachelor of Science in Journalism from Southern Illinois University.

SPEECHES AND APPEARANCES

Mr. Milano is an in-demand speaker. For bookings, contact

Contemporary Issues Agency

809 Turnberry Drive, Waunakee, WI 53597-2256
Phone: 800-843-2179
Fax: 608-849-6311
www.CIAspeakers.com
Info@CIAspeakers.com